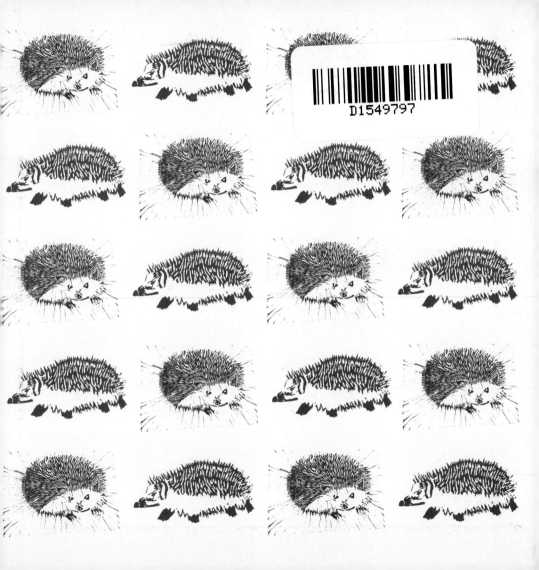

D1549797

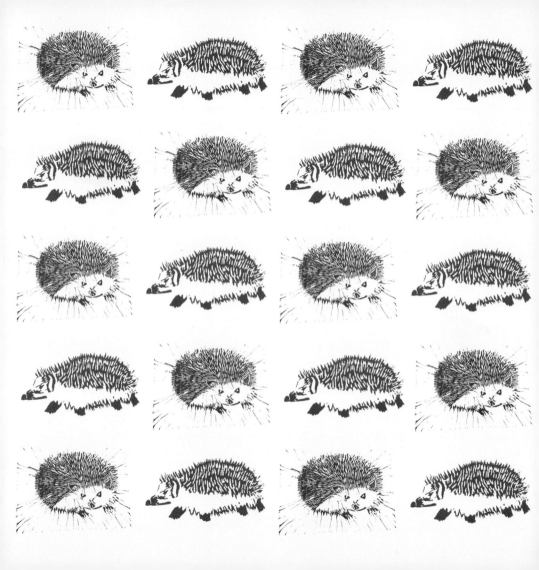

The Hedgehog Book

by Hugh Warwick

Series editor Jane Russ

GRAFFEG

Dedication

To Anne – the badger that brings this hedgehog such joy.

Contents

What Is a Hedgehog?

What Is a Hedgehog?

A hedgehog is a mammal – Britain's only spiny mammal – and its closest relatives are the shrew and the mole.

This means it is not closely related to porcupines, which are rodents, or to the tenrecs from Madagascar, convergent evolution gifting them similar modes of defence.

There is just one species of hedgehog living in the wild in the United Kingdom – the Western European hedgehog (*Erinaceus europaeus*). However, there are 14 other species living across Europe, Asia and Africa. There are a few people who keep some of the African species as pets in this country, but those cannot tolerate our climate. The hedgehogs that live in New Zealand are ex-pats, having been requested by colonialists in the 19th century to make them feel more at home.

The name for the animal is one of the easiest to unpick, as they like to hog the hedge, although the 'hog' is probably more related to the snuffling noises they make as they push through the undergrowth. Some have suggested that it could be related to the fact bald ones look rather like a young boar, or that they might taste like pork.

Other names used on these islands include urchin, a name that predates hedgehog. This comes from the Norman *herichon* and is reflected in

A tenrec from Madagascar.

the presence of sea-urchins. Less charitably, there are Celtic names that all translate as the 'horrible one': *grainneog* (Irish), *crainneag* (Scottish Gaelic) and *draenog* (Welsh).

The life cycle of a hedgehog has been determined in large part by its protective coat of spines. The spines are made of keratin, the same stuff as fingernails, and are, in effect, modified hair. They cover the back and sides of the animal, but the face and tummy are covered in a fairly sparse fur – if the spines spread that far, the hedgehog's famous defence of rolling up would be impossible. At around 2cm long, they are far shorter than the long spines on a porcupine. They are held in the hedgehog's skin by a bulb, and have a narrow neck close to the surface, allowing them to function as effective shock absorbers as well as their obvious defensive role.

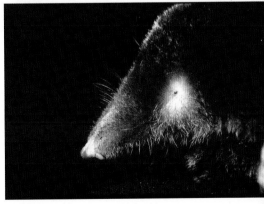

Above: A shrew and a mole, the hedgehog's closest relatives.

Functioning as shock absorbers means that, if a hedgehog falls, its spines won't be driven into its body, something that has encouraged hedgehogs to some occasionally alarming feats of climbing. Tales of hedgehogs being found in first-floor bedrooms, having clambered up the stairs, are nothing to the story of a hedgehog and a rat found having a fight in the Virginia creeper outside a first-floor bedroom window.

Sometimes a hedgehog with alopecia

Above: A hedgehog with alopecia.

turns up at a rescue centre, and these, while obviously very vulnerable, provide an insight into what a hedgehog looks like under that covering of 5-7,000 spines.

The impact the spines have on the life cycle of a hedgehog comes from the compromise they provide between insulation from the cold and protection from predators. The transformation

Hedgehog spines.

of fur into spines, over millennia of natural selection, reduced the animal's capacity to tolerate cold and has led it to develop the technique of hibernation. The lack of insulation means that hedgehogs would need to keep eating during the coldest time of the year, but the hedgehog's natural diet is heavily dominated by invertebrates and, as the weather gets colder, these exothermic (cold-blooded) animals tend to hide away beyond the reach of their limited digging ability.

What Do Hedgehogs Eat?

What Do Hedgehogs Eat?

Hedgehogs are carnivores. Until recently they were stuffed into the taxonomic order of the insectivores, however, taxonomists felt that the members of this group were too varied for it to be useful and hedgehogs have been moved to the Eulipotyphlan order. Now, insectivore is a term that describes, quite accurately, a hedgehog's diet. They mainly eat macroinvertebrates, the larger bugs and beasts. Eulipotyphlan, on the other hand, translates as 'truly fat and blind' which is unfortunate. It is actually a reference to their caecum, part of their intestine.

Over the years hedgehogs have been credited with all sorts of unlikely dietary eccentricities and these will be discussed later. For now, what they actually eat in the wild is the focus. This has been studied through the hard work of both faecal and stomach content analysis. Derek Yalden analysed the stomachs of 137 dead hedgehogs and found that in 73% were the remains of beetles. Next most popular items were earwigs, caterpillars, millipedes and worms. Of course, hedgehogs are famous for eating slugs, and they were the next most populous content, at 23%. These were hedgehogs that had been killed by gamekeepers and reflect the diet of hedgehogs on the land they were found.

Faecal analysis from gardens generated some alarming results. Rather than looking through a microscope researchers are now able to look at the DNA and from this identify what species have been eaten, which included pigs and cows! After a moment of panic, it was realised that this was just picking up

the evidence of meaty pet food being put out for them.

A question worth considering is how much of a choice do hedgehogs make regarding their food? Are they just eating what is common? To some extent that seems to be the case, though they select slugs over snails, due to shells, and they select millipedes over woodlice, probably due to their more astringent taste.

An interesting impact of strong-tasting morsels is the act of self-anointing, where a hedgehog that has chewed or licked something with a strong flavour or scent will work up a froth of saliva and then stretch and spread this foam across their spines. This would seem to be some sort of scent-dispersal technique,

or possibly scent disguise, but it remains not fully understood and as it has also been stimulated by distilled water, the true cause is a bit of a mystery.

Like us, they will consume things that are not good for them. They are lactose intolerant, but they just don't know that, so will drink milk to their detriment. They will eat mealworms to the exclusion of pretty much everything else, which has led some to demand that mealworms should be removed from all foods left out for hedgehogs for fear that this causes a mineral imbalance known as metabolic bone disease.

Hedgehog Life

Hedgehog Life

Let us start the lifecycle of the hedgehog as it emerges from hibernation. This is one of the most vulnerable times of the year. Hibernation uses fat reserves that have been stored during the previous autumn and early spring is a challenge, though it is possible to become too fat, as this poor chap has found out having been cared for by an inexperienced, and overly generous, rehabilitator.

Hedgehogs usually start to be seen in March, with most of them out of hibernation by the beginning of April, though anecdotally there is evidence that hedgehogs are being more active during the winter than previously, and that this may be a result of a changing climate.

There is a very clear difference in the time of emergence between males

and females. Research undertaken by Pat Morris looked at the sex ratios of hedgehogs found throughout the year, and what this shows relates

clearly to their lifecycle. In spring there are far more male hedgehogs seen about – 64:36 male:female. In the middle of the year the ratio is 46:54 before before swinging back to 25:75 in the autumn.

Why would this be the case? Males emerge earlier from hibernation because they have mating in mind – they are also more active and therefore more likely to be found.

They are scouting the landscape for females with whom they hope to stake a claim, and by the end of the year, well, the males' involvement in reproduction ends almost as soon as it begins. Females, however, are tied to the young and stay out of hibernation for longer in order to give themselves time to feed and build up fat reserves, which will be depleted as they feed their offspring.

Hibernation

Hibernation is a remarkable adaptation. There are few true hibernators in Britain – dormice and bats are the others. Stimulated by changes in temperature and food availability, the hedgehog builds a more robust and secure nest than either the day nest or the nursing nest. It is known as a hibernaculum and is crucial to the success of this challenging time of year.

The ability to ride out the roughest weather in what appears to be a deep sleep must surely appeal to many and it is a capacity that has fascinated people for many years – not least because if humanity is going to spread itself beyond this one planet, people will need to do something like hibernation for the many years of travel.

Interestingly, desert-dwelling

hedgehogs carry out a similar activity – or rather lack of activity – but during the heat of the year, known as aestivation, *hiber* being the Latin for winter, while *aester* means heat.

The real fascination, though, started long before space travel was an idea. Consider an animal that appears to be dead – or as close to dead as is possible – for a large portion of the year. How could that not amaze? And it may well be one of the reasons for such interest from the earliest civilisations, as seen in the artefacts they left behind.

Hibernation is not sleep – while sleep is necessary to survival, a hedgehog, should it be warm and fed, will quite happily not hibernate, and in New Zealand, for example, where 'our' hedgehogs were exported in the 19th

century, they hardly hibernate at all, as the conditions are so clement year round.

But when hibernation is called upon, it is a profoundly different event to sleep. While sleeping, a hedgehog's body temperature might drop a degree or two, but in deep hibernation it drops to match the environment and both their breathing and heartbeat almost stop as they reduce their metabolic activity by around 98%. Only when the weather becomes extremely cold does the body kick in to produce a little heat to keep the animal from freezing.

This explains why one of the most crucial components of a successful hibernation is a good and sturdy hibernaculum. It is vital that the hedgehog is insulated from the extremes of winter weather, both hot and cold.

That might seem counterintuitive, but it is important that hedgehogs do not get too warm while hibernating – this is to do with the different sorts of fat that the hedgehog lays down during the autumn.

There are two varieties of fat, white and brown. White is the basic energy source that keeps the hedgehog ticking over at 2% of its usual output, but it is the brown fat that is fascinating. This is stored around their shoulders and is the 'starter motor' to kick the body into life. The problem with a poorly insulated nest is that occasional warm winter days can trigger the hedgehog into waking up before the winter is truly over and, depending on their fat stores, the more this happens, the more likely it is that the reserves will be depleted. Then the unfortunate animal will find resurrection impossible.

How much does a hedgehog need to weigh to survive hibernation? This is a fascinating question that generates quite a degree of discussion every autumn, the reason being that the answer is not simple and that there are lots of people who want to help, but also want a simple answer. People want to help because they can. The hedgehog, unlike almost every other animal in the UK, lacks a fight or flight response, thanks to its defensive coat of spines. There will be more about the amazing work of hedgehog hospitals later, but for now, the thorny issue of when to intervene needs to be addressed.

The facts as we know them are that any hedgehog entering hibernation weighing less than 450g is unlikely to survive. That does not mean that the optimal weight for entering hibernation is 450g, of course. If a hedgehog is too fat, however, and this does happen with animals in captivity, they are unable to roll up properly to defend themselves, indicating there must surely be an optimal weight.

As with most of life, simple answers do not exist. You can have a very fit hedgehog weighing 450g that will sail through hibernation absolutely fine, and you can have an unfit hedgehog weighing 800g that will die because it is in poor condition. But for members of the public to help hedgehogs, there is a need to give a figure under which hedgehogs should be brought in and fed up until they are at a suitable weight for the winter.

This has led to an absurd situation, with one rescue calling for all hedgehogs weighing under 900g to be brought in for feeding up and

another calling for all hedgehogs weighing over 950g to be brought in to go on a diet, as they would be too fat to curl up effectively. A 50g window – the Goldilocks weight – is ridiculous and brings the work of sensible carers into disrepute by association.

The British Hedgehog Preservation Society advice is simple: hedgehogs should normally be rescued at weights less than 450g in October-February (depending on the weather and the frequency with which they are seen at feeding stations). Rescuing when they weigh more than 500g is unnecessary, based on weight alone, at any time of the year, but it is important to remember that weight is irrelevant if the hedgehog is out during the day unnecessarily or appears ill or injured.

There is growing evidence that 'rescue' at weights above 600g, based on weight alone, is counterproductive and strongly discouraged. Bringing a healthy hedgehog into a rescue is stressful for the hedgehog and parasite burdens can be amplified, causing serious problems for the animal. There are further risks involved with being in close proximity to other hedgehogs with possible contagious conditions.

Left: Hibernation nests are built with leaves combed into layers underneath a structure.

If a hedgehog is out during the day or appears ill or injured in any way it should be brought into care regardless of weight, unless it is a female hedgehog nest building during breeding season or taking a break from the nest. These will be adult hedgehogs and move with purpose, out for short spells at a time.

It is also known that very fat hedgehogs, on release into the wild in the spring and having been kept awake all winter, lose weight rapidly.

So, the nest – the hibernaculum – is crucial. And amazing. It is made up of vegetation, like a usual day nest, but is far more robust. Pat Morris conducted the first ever study of these structures and found that the walls, layers of tightly packed leaves, were often up to 20cm thick.

Leaves are needed for a hedgehog to be successful in hibernating and this is an argument for not being too 'tidy' in your garden. Not just any leaves will do – too small and they do not provide the insulating cover, too large and they do not compact so easily. Imagine oak, hazel and lime, that is about right. The layering is achieved by the hedgehog pushing into the bundle of vegetation and then rotating, the spines acting as a comb to pull the leaves into order.

The other key feature is a structure under which the nest can be built. This will usually be a patch of brambles or the bottom of a hedge, but can also be under a shed or even in a specially made hedgehog house. The normal distribution of hedgehogs is dictated by their ability to access leaves, so the tree line is a good gauge as to whether there will

be any hedgehogs. This is not always the case, as the hedgehog nesting in rabbit holes in the Outer Hebrides has shown.

While hibernation is vital in ensuring hedgehogs a chance of surviving winter throughout most of their range, there is increasing evidence that they do not stay locked in hibernation the whole winter through. Recent research has shown that most hedgehogs change their hibernaculum at least once during the winter, and a study in Denmark showed some hedgehogs changing their nests on eight occasions.

Because there was not the same level of attention paid to hedgehog behaviour in the past, it is impossible to know whether this level of activity is what has always happened, or is a comment on changing climate.

One idea suggested, again by Pat Morris, was that the date of emergence of hedgehogs from hibernation could give a measure of changing climate, arguing that if the data he collected of first sightings during the 1960s was compared to similar data from today, we might see that they are emerging sooner.

The study received thousands of reports of the first sightings of hedgehogs across the country, but interestingly was unable to find any clear evidence in the quite messy data. This is one of the great things about science – you get to test your ideas and sometimes what you think will happen, doesn't!

Given that many thousands of hedgehogs are taken into care each autumn and winter – the fact we do not know how many is in itself worrying – it was necessary to find out whether they were being released with the ability to survive, or whether they were being kept for the benefit of those who wanted to care for wildlife, also unknown prior to the research. Fortunately, it transpires that hedgehogs kept in over winter and then released behave like normal hedgehogs. They are not in any way granted immortality, so some do die, and it is possible that in the first few weeks a few more die than would be expected of the population as a whole. But in the end, caring for and releasing hedgehogs in need of help is a good thing.

Emerging from hibernation in the spring, there are two things that drive hedgehogs – food and sex.

How Do Hedgehogs Mate?

This is a frequently asked question and is most simply answered, carefully. Yes, that can sound like a joke, but it is also a true representation of what happens.

So clearly has this been a problem to comprehend that Aristotle described mating taking place with both animals standing upright, belly to belly. As with many of these erroneous statements on natural history, it was treated with great authority and repeated as fact down the centuries, despite it never having been witnessed.

Actually, mating takes place in the same manner as other four-legged animals, just with that extra element to overcome.

Females come into breeding condition soon after they emerge from hibernation, by the end of

March or early April.

During the breeding season there is a chance to identify male and female hedgehogs thanks to the behaviour exhibited during courtship.

Usually it is impossible to be sure whether a hedgehog seen out in the garden is male or female without a look at its genitals. This requires the hedgehog to be picked up and then encouraged to unroll, as it will probably have curled up at that point. A swift look at the underside will give you an inkling of who you have in your hands – if the animal appears to have a tummy button, it is a male, though this can cause the hedgehog stress, so is best avoided.

At the April-June peak of the mating season, however, one or more males will be attracted to a female that is fertile. Males will tend to fight

between themselves and it can be an ugly squabble, with the more dominant tending to barge and roll the subordinate out of the way. When one is left he will begin what is known as the 'hedgehog carousel' – he circles the female, trying to get behind her. She turns to face him, occasionally emitting a plosive sneeze of a noise, which can make him jump back.

The carousel can last for more than an hour, and it is at this time that the sexes are easily identifiable, as

It is quite possible to stroke a happy hedgehog. When they are relaxed, all the spines lie in the same direction.

it is the male who is circling. Mating cannot take place while the female frowns, and she spends a lot of time during this ritual frowning.

On a hedgehog the frown muscle stretches all the way from above the nose to the tail and, when nervous, rather than immediately curling up into a ball, it frowns. The contraction of the panniculus carnosus along with the muscle attachments at the base of each of the spines causes them to erect and pull forward, protecting the face.

It is quite possible to stroke a happy hedgehog. When they are relaxed, all the spines lie in the same direction, and when the female is relaxed, mating has a greater chance of success. But courtship is not a guarantee to a successful

mating and quiet observations of the process have found that considerably less than 10% of attempts are consummated. Hedgehogs are promiscuous, with both males and females courting and mating with many individuals.

When mating has occurred, that is the end of the male involvement. Any images of 'happy hedgehog families' with a mum and dad are drawn from the same natural history expertise as exhibited by Aristotle.

Pregnancy lasts for around 34 days, but there is a degree of variation in this. Towards the end of this period the female will build a nursery nest, which is more robust than a typical day nest and, like the hibernaculum, tucked out of the way.

Now to an eye-watering fact: baby hedgehogs are born with spines. However, and this is a crucial bit of wonderful evolution, newborns are covered in oedemic, fluid-filled skin. The fluid is quickly absorbed after birth, allowing the spines to emerge far faster than could ever be achieved by growth.

The four or five young are born very pale, the skin not darkening for around a week, and while the eyes do not open until the third week, they are capable of limited defence very early on, lowering their heads when feeling threatened. Full rolling up is not possible until they have developed the necessary muscles and this can take three months.

The first set of 100 or so spines are white and do not change colour, supplemented over time by darker spines growing amongst them. By the time they leave the nest, juvenile hedgehogs will have around 3000 spines. Pat Morris counted the spines on a sample of hedgehogs and found there to be an average of about 5000 per adult.

Newborn hedgehogs can be eaten by their mother if she or the nest are disturbed, but after a few days they are secure from that fate and she will even carry them to a new nest site if necessary. By about four weeks they will start to explore and this can result in one of the most adorable images: a mother leading a small train of youngsters as she heads out on a nocturnal ramble. By six weeks the hedgehogs are independent and able to live alone.

It seems most likely that female hedgehogs do not successfully breed

in their first full year and there is evidence that points towards the reproductive burden being placed on more mature animals. Whether they can manage to breed twice in one year is interesting and frequently thought to be the reason for the flush of juveniles too small to survive hibernation found in the autumn. It is also possible that these unfortunate young are the results of the first breeding attempts by females taking place later in the year as they build up size and strength.

How Many Hedgehogs Are There?

How Many Hedgehogs Are There?

The hedgehog population of the United Kingdom is suffering a serious decline. Absolute numbers of hedgehogs in the country remain in the realms of educated guesswork. What we have to measure is the rate of change over time, and with considerable robustness we now know that since the year 2000 urban hedgehog numbers are down by around a third, and rural numbers down by over a half, in less than 20 years.

But what about the decade before? The problem we have is that there were no similarly robust surveys being undertaken, and so we have to extrapolate, use anecdotes, and try not to leap on the figure that was published in 1969, which suggests that there were 36.5 million hedgehogs in 1950. This is guesswork, an extrapolation from a summer evening walk around Kew Gardens.

The figure is unreliable, but it is worth considering how difficult it is to count hedgehogs. A survey of the imported hedgehogs on North Ronaldsay, Orkney, proved a case in point. The research topic seemed straightforward enough – to find out how many there were and whether they were the cause for the decline in the breeding success of ground-nesting birds.

The island is largely small, five miles long and one mile wide at the extremes, and largely flat, but still it proved hard to find these cryptic nocturnal creatures. It is relatively easy for birdwatchers, but they are dealing with creatures that are mostly diurnal and frequently advertise their presence with song.

Ecologist Carly Pettett radio
tracking hedgehogs for her PhD.

To prepare a scientific case for the conservation of hedgehogs it is necessary to base action on not the absolute number that are present but on the rate of change over time. This gives a metric we can use to see whether there is a problem or whether an intervention is working.

So how to do that? We have a number of surveys that run – some that are a little gruesome.

Hedgehogs have not learned how to cross roads more carefully. The reason why fewer hedgehogs are seen killed on the road is because there are fewer trying to cross the road. This gives us a way of measuring the relative abundance in an area and is part of the People's Trust for Endangered Species survey called 'Mammals on Road'.

Their project called 'Living with Mammals' also gives us an insight into where hedgehogs are being seen – as does the work done by the indefatigable British Trust for Ornithology observers as they count the wildlife in their gardens.

These data are combined into a biannual report called 'State of Britain's Hedgehogs', and this gives an ever more accurate insight into how populations have changed. Educated guesswork does, however, have a place in trying to give an overall view of the way the population of the nation's favourite animal has changed over time, from which it is not unreasonable to suppose a 90-95% decline in hedgehog numbers since the end of the Second World War.

One of the largest problems hedgehogs face has been revealed during research, and that is 'habitat fragmentation' – the splitting up of our landscape into smaller pockets of land which might in themselves be wonderful hedgehog habitat, but are too small to support a viable population. Hedgehogs need to travel far further than their little legs would suggest was necessary.

For example, while out radio tracking hedgehogs – a very effective tool to monitor their behaviour whereby a small radio transmitter is attached to the hedgehog's spines and its signal picked up by an antennae carried by the researcher – it is not unknown for the hedgehogs to travel 2km in a single night.

Other work has shown that a male hedgehog can cover an entire 18-hole golf course in less than two weeks, leading to the researcher

estimating home ranges for males to be around 30ha and females around 10ha.

From this, a modelling exercise was undertaken where all the best data were collected and fed into a computer to try and work out what area a population of hedgehogs needed in order to thrive. This is known as a minimum viable population analysis and the results were startling. Imagine an island – and in effect many parts of our country are 'islands' – surrounded not by the sea, but by barriers of roads, fences, walls, canals and industrial estates. The island needs to be at least 90ha to support the minimum population of 32 hedgehogs. If the 'island' is smaller, or there are too few hedgehogs, then they will eventually disappear from the area, unless replenished.

Threats to Hedgehogs

Threats to Hedgehogs

Identifying the fact that hedgehog numbers are declining is only the start, of course. We have to work out why.

As the data reveal, there seems to be a clear difference in the fate of urban and rural hedgehogs; it is not the way around one would think! While we most often see hedgehogs in a suburban setting, because that is where most of us are, if you were to think of a 'natural' home for a hedgehog it would probably be amidst the hedges of farmland.

So why is it that hedgehogs fare so poorly in our farmed landscape? As with all wildlife, the requirements for survival are straightforward: food, water, shelter and the ability to move freely.

Industrial agriculture requires the removal of competition, and so the macroinvertebrates that might feed on a crop are exterminated, and with them hedgehog food is gone, as well as that for the bat, bird, amphibian and reptile too. This is not hyperbole – there is a growing body of evidence that shows a loss of insects across the industrial agricultural landscapes of the world. In Germany in 2017 they published the results of a 25-year-long study looking at the biomass of flying insects in protected areas, which was down by 75%. Remember that this was in the areas of the land that were protected.

To let those bugs flourish also requires a diversity of plant life, so even in green pastures there is a problem because these fields are predominantly just perennial rye – all of the wild flowers consigned to the margins.

The field margins – famous in this country for often being the hedges that gave our hedgehog the name – have long since lost their glory. There is now around 300,000km less hedgerow in the UK than there was at 'peak hedge', and so much of what is left is in poor condition. Initially the threat was that of subsidy-driven treats to encourage active removal of hedges, increasing field size and thereby maximising financial returns.

Now the greatest threat is neglect.

Hedgerow neglect, in the current environment, is understandable. To maintain a hedgerow in good working order it needs to be layed – the wonderful art of half cutting down the trees of a hedgeline and weaving them into a stock-proof barrier. But this is expensive. Very roughly, it costs £12.50 for each metre of hedge managed this way. A tractor-borne flail costs around 6p for every metre managed.

There are far too few eagle owls for them to be a cause of concern

There is no escaping another cause of the decline in rural hedgehogs, and that is the badger. This magnificent creature is the only natural predator of the hedgehog that remains on these islands – there are far too few eagle owls for them to be a cause of concern. But the problem for hedgehogs is not simply one of being eaten; in fact, that is probably a relatively small component.

Badgers and hedgehogs have what is know as an 'asymmetric intraguild predatory relationship'. This means that they are primarily competitors for the same food – in this case macroinvertebrates. And as we know already, populations of these animals are declining dramatically. Badgers are more efficient predators of these animals and therefore outcompete hedgehogs.

Our best understanding is that when the wider ecosystem becomes degraded, the relationship between these two species shifts from one of competition to one of predation. This does not mean that the loss of hedgehogs from our rural landscape can be blamed on badgers eating them all. This is an ecological problem and these are rarely 'black and white'.

It is also known that badgers create a 'landscape of fear', which can curtail the ability of hedgehogs to move freely. Active badger setts and latrines along field margins, the route a hedgehog will take to disperse, tend to send adventurous hedgehogs back the way they came. They find the landscape fragmented by the presence of badgers.

Above: Adult female eagle owl bringing
in the hedgehog as pray for her
offspring, Lower Saxony, Germany.

Fragmentation is at the heart of the problems faced by suburban hedgehogs too, though here the cause is often more obvious, should we choose to look. It is possible to make the most perfectly wildlife-friendly garden and bask in the flurry of life as birds, bats, bees and butterflies make use of the work. One person complained that they had done all that they could, yet they had no hedgehogs. When asked what they had around the garden, the answer was revealing: 'a damn good wall, keeps the neighbour's cat out.'

Loss of habitat in the suburban environment is also a problem – new houses being built, gardens becoming patios and decking – but it is possible, as we shall see, to accommodate hedgehogs in this world, should we care enough to do so.

It is impossible to ignore the most stereotypical fate of the hedgehog – being killed by cars. The tragedy, now, though, is that relatively few hedgehogs are seen squashed – and, as we have seen, this is one of the most effective measures for population change. Remember, hedgehogs are not getting any cleverer at crossing the road. If they are not found dead there, there are likely to be very few in the surrounds.

The most recent research, analysing records from across the years and around the country, suggests that in excess of 100,000 hedgehogs are killed on the roads each year. Given that their total population is something south of a million, this is clearly of conservation concern.

In addition to killing hedgehogs, roads have another impact on

their ability to thrive, as busy roads present barriers to movement. Radio-tracking studies have shown that hedgehogs simply don't bother trying to cross the busiest of roads, and the tendency to reinforce the central boundary of roads with concrete walls has shifted many from being difficult to cross to being utterly impassable.

There are other anthropogenic hazards that hedgehogs have to contend with in our suburban spaces. Water – vital, of course, to life, but also a potential problem. Hedgehogs can swim, but they can't swim forever, so any water body needs to have some way the hedgehog, and other animals, can escape. This could simply be a ramp in your ornamental pond – if it is a wildlife pond it will already have a beach or shallow end that will enable animals to come to the water to drink – and allow a hedgehog that has accidentally fallen in to escape. Swimming pools are more of a problem, though not as common in themselves. Here a good cover will help, and there are even some wildlife-friendly structures that can be added to ladders to allow wildlife to escape.

Falling into things is unfortunately something that hedgehogs have a tendency to do. Being nocturnal and prone to snuffling around being lead by their nose, hazards such as open drains or newly dug foundations can create a death trap.

Now, consider the best possible hedgehog home – a large bundle

of dried leaves surrounded by a supportive structure of thin sticks, in turn covered by larger pieces of wood, and on to decent-sized logs. So protective, so secure, so warm... and soon to be so hot. Of course, this is a bonfire. And every autumn, in particular in the run up to Bonfire Night, the British Hedgehog Preservation Society has to remind people to not incinerate hedgehogs and other wildlife sheltering in these great creations. The easiest solution is to build a bonfire on the day it is to be lit, while hedgehogs are busy sleeping elsewhere. If it needs to be built in advance, gently lift the structure with the blunt end of a rake and use a torch to see if any life has taken up residence. If it is to be a mammoth community affair, consider putting a barrier around it, tight to the ground and taut so that hedgehogs won't be able to become tangled.

Becoming caught in netting is a terrible fate for a hedgehog. Their spines, so good at keeping them safe, here pose a real problem. Once a hedgehog has pushed, accidentally, into netting, reversing is not an option, and when it feels the constriction it senses a threat and rolls up, exacerbating the situation. Being caught leaves them vulnerable to thirst and hunger, of course, but the real worry comes from flies. As the day warms up, so flies begin to sniff around for places to lay eggs, and a hedgehog caught in a net is a perfect place. Once eggs have been laid, and if no rescue is forthcoming, they hatch and the resulting maggots start to eat. This is known as flystrike and is one of the most distressing problems hedgehog rescuers have to deal with.

Litter has been found to cause real problems too. From elastic bands to pots of ice cream, a hedgehog's nose-down snuffling leaves them at risk of getting caught. The BHPS has been sent many images of hedgehogs caught in such circumstances – including a series of pictures of hedgehogs with their heads caught inside McDonald's ice cream cups. The design of the containers for the McFlurry meant that a hedgehog, still unaware of their lactose intolerant status, would push its head beyond the hole in the lid to lap the sweet and fatty residue, but then find its retreat halted by the spines holding it inside the small hole.

The BHPS launched a campaign through which, eventually, after eight years of lobbying, letter-writing and meetings, McDonald's relented and redesigned the lid. While that is wonderful news and real proof of people power, it is depressing that it took the corporation so long to consider reducing their impact on these precious animals.

There is another threat that is probably the most distressing of all – and one that appears in the press most years – when gangs of kids are found to have kicked a hedgehog to death. The sadness for the animal has also to be extended to these children, because such callous violence is an indication of a deeply sad and damaged life.

Ways We Can Help

Ways We Can Help

The British Hedgehog Preservation Society and the People's Trust for Endangered Species have been collaborating and running the Hedgehog Street campaign since 2011.

The essence of the campaign is simple. While a hedgehog, small, cute and bumbling, might look as if it fits easily into a garden or two, the reality is that they need far greater areas to be able to thrive. Not just a hedgehog garden, but an entire hedgehog street is necessary.

To begin with, the campaign printed material to send to the 'Hedgehog Champions' who registered – 2000 packs were printed and there was worry that the office might have boxes left over. There need not have been any worry. The national interest in hedgehogs is so strong that within weeks they had all gone and the campaign was moved almost entirely onto the web, where now there are over 70,000 households signed-up. The website might not match other social media behemoths like Facebook, but it has become a very busy place where people share experiences and ideas, learn how best to encourage hedgehogs into their gardens and find neighbours who are also involved. The new mobile app is also drawing people into a shared world of hedgehog lovers.

One of the most fascinating features is the Big Hedgehog Map – this wonderful resource allows Hedgehog Champions to plot hedgehog sightings and hedgehog holes on a national map. While it might not be the most scientific of samples, measuring, as it does, where keen

people are as well as hedgehogs, it does provide a very useful tool. For example, when wanting to know if there is any chance of attracting hedgehogs to a garden, it is worth looking to see if hedgehogs have been seen in the area. Now, if there are no hedgehog sightings, that should not prevent work being done, but it can help manage expectations.

So, what work needs to be done? As is clear, the most important thing we can do is 'think hedgehog'. Take a good look around the garden, if that is what you are managing, and see firstly if a hedgehog can actually get in!

It has been joked that the hedgehog is becoming an honorary bird, due to the vast amount of effort the RSPB has been putting into fundraising using this mammal. But they are not a bird, and they cannot fly. They need to be able to get into a garden and for that they need a hole. Now, it does not need to be a very big hole, just 13cm square, about the size of a CD case. Unfortunately, these are drifting out of fashion, so the measurement will have to do.

There are a few instances where a hole like this can be a problem. If you or your neighbour owns a miniature dachshund or small tortoise, this will not work. Likewise, there are concerns from people who have gardens full of vegetables that are surrounded by rabbits.

Otherwise, a hole is a good thing, but talk to your neighbour, and then get them to talk to their neighbour, and onwards, spreading hedgehog love down the street. Hedgehog street parties have become quite a

thing, as have hedgehog cakes and bunting too. There is a wonderful chance for a community to come together over something that helps both hedgehogs and people and new friendships have been made.

There are some communities that have taken this even further – Kirtlington, north Oxfordshire, is a case in point. The Kirtlington Wildlife and Conservation Society had received a few talks about hedgehogs and habitat fragmentation and decided to put the ideas into action. They got hold of a detailed map of the village and worked out the minimum number of holes the walled gardens needed to open up the space for hedgehogs, and then they set to work.

The innovation was amazing. When one garden was found to be nearly a metre lower than its neighbour, a stone staircase was built. And the first night the staircase was in action, a hedgehog came through the hole

at the top and surveyed the scene before sashaying down the stairs with great aplomb, all captured on a well-placed trail camera.

The top-ten tips for helping hedgehogs have been condensed into a very popular leaflet from Hedgehog Street, and along with making holes, keeping ponds safe, lifting up netting and being careful with bonfires there are six other simple steps to making

sure you have a hedgehog-friendly garden.

It might seem odd to think about growing specific wild plants for hedgehogs, as they don't tend to eat vegetation, but a wild patch with brambles and 'weeds' is a wonderful resource, especially if you can include insect-attracting plants, as insects lay eggs which grow into hedgehog food. A log pile, for example, is brilliant, as it also provides a structure in or under which a hedgehog can build a nest.

Putting food and water out for hedgehogs can be a lifeline, especially water during hot and dry spells – shallow dishes of water can become the first place a hedgehog visits in the garden. The food advice used to be restricted to meaty pet food, though not fish, but now there is also a wide range of specially produced hedgehog foods available. The extra step is to create a feeding station – a place where you can encourage the hedgehogs and discourage other beasts. This is at its simplest a box placed upside down over the food, with, obviously, a hole (13cm across) cut into the side. To further focus who is going to be fed, put a brick on top to stop foxes knocking it over

and consider creating a partition inside the box, with the food tucked out of the way behind it – this will stop the inquisitive paws of pussy cats reaching inside and can also discourage rats.

There is little to commend the use of toxic chemicals in your garden, the insecticides, herbicides, fungicides and molluscicides all have the power to injure or kill hedgehogs, and worse still is the combined effect, though no one has ever tested what happens when hedgehogs are fed a combined dose of rat poison, slug pellet and glyphosate. While the main worry is about the unintended impact of these poisons on hedgehogs, consider also that many of them are being used specifically to remove hedgehog food from the garden.

Slugs can be evil, gnawing at seedlings and stripping the potential from new growth, but around 50% of all slugs are in fact detritivores – they are the ones that eat dead plant material and help generate fertile soil – and they are being killed by slug pellets too. There are creative solutions to the menace that slugs present, though some of the folk remedies seem not to stand up to scrutiny. Consider alternatives and that will encourage healthy hedgehogs, who also happen to like eating slugs.

One of the most tragic sights are the hedgehogs that have been caught by garden machinery, and one of the worst culprits is the strimmer. The speed with which it is possible to skim along the base of a hedge, removing the weedy growth, can feel wonderfully liberating, but remember, hedgehogs do not have a fight or flight response. The impending threat of a loud machine to their day-nest snooze will cause the hedgehog to curl up and wait for it to pass, and while this might work well with a fox, with a strimmer or mower the results can be disastrous. How to solve that problem? Take a little more time and run a foot along the base of the hedge before you start – a gentle kick is far more preferable to a hedgehog than the alternative.

Hedgehog homes – should you build or buy one? If your garden is already wildlife friendly, there is probably no need to have a hedgehog house. If there are patches of brambles and a log pile, what more could a hedgehog need? But if you are a bit tidy, then there is good evidence that a hedgehog house will work.

The presence of pets and, surprisingly, badgers, did not seem to stop hedgehogs taking up residence.

The Hedgehog Street campaign's Hedgehog Housing Census received an amazing response, with over 5,000 people sending in information about the hedgehog houses in their gardens, what they were made of, where they were sited and whether they were used.

The results were interesting, with hedgehogs seeming to prefer homemade houses over bought ones. Now this could be that people who made houses did so in response to seeing a hedgehog in their garden, and that people with bought houses were either in receipt of a gift or were just hoping it might attract a hedgehog. The results also showed that patience is a virtue, as hedgehogs can take quite some time

to get used to a new potential nest site, though putting a little bedding, food and water in the garden or in the house along with more bedding seems to speed up acceptance.

Shaded areas of the back garden are preferable, but interestingly houses situated less than 5m from the human house were used most frequently, indicating how accustomed they are to human activity. The presence of pets and, more surprisingly, badgers, did not seem to stop hedgehogs taking up residence.

Helping hedgehogs is not just restricted to our gardens. Hedgehog Street has established an in-depth Hedgehog Ecology and Management for Practioners course that has been run all over the country, introducing land managers, ecological consultants, council workers and planners to the needs of hedgehogs.

Hedgehogs on agricultural land have suffered some of the steepest declines in numbers and Hedgehog Street has begun to offer specialist help for the farming community as well. Much of this focuses on the need to plant, keep and manage hedgerows and wilder parts of the farmed landscape. There is little chance a hedgehog will find much fun in the middle of a field of oilseed rape. Industrial crops like this require an average of 17 applications of agrochemical per crop, and also require that fields be as large as possible to maximise financial returns.

The final team of people that the campaign is reaching out to is the developers. There are plans to build hundreds of thousands of new homes across the country, and these homes have the potential to destroy good wildlife, and hedgehog habitats in particular. By presenting a detailed guide as to how to minimise the damage, it is possible that developers could be persuaded to give just a little thought to the hedgehogs on their land.

The most effective work with developers has come from a change.org petition calling for all new developments to be built with hedgehog highways as standard, which is so much easier than retrofitting holes in fences. The first developer to leap at the chance of becoming famously hedgehog friendly were Bovis Homes.

Hedgehog Rescuers

Hedgehog Rescuers

Unlike any other British animal, the hedgehog is regularly taken into care by amateurs with a view to fixing them up and releasing them back into the wild. The BHPS has a list of over 600 people and organisations to whom a caller can be directed and the carers range dramatically in scale and expertise. There are wildlife hospitals with professional staff who deal with thousands of casualties (of all species) each year, all the way to the lone operator who might overwinter a hedgehog or two in a box, keeping it fed and preparing it for release back into the wild.

The differing levels of expertise is behind the call from some to have all wildlife rescues licensed, because there are some who simply do not do a good job. However, licensing would require there to be a set of guidelines as to best practice that could be agreed upon, and this is difficult to achieve.

Carers will develop their own way of doing things and risk becoming dogmatic. An accepted hierarchy of evidence that ranges from 'expert opinion' to 'cohort studies' and 'randomised control trials', with expert opinion being on the lowest rung and the most prone to bias, clearly reveals the differences carers have in approaching hedgehogs. Unfortunately, there is very little chance that the science will ever be affordable to do, so whatever guidelines are produced will have to be based on a review of expert opinion.

This is not to say that there are not carers out there who are not doing an amazing job. For example, Vale Wildlife Rescue, near Tewkesbury,

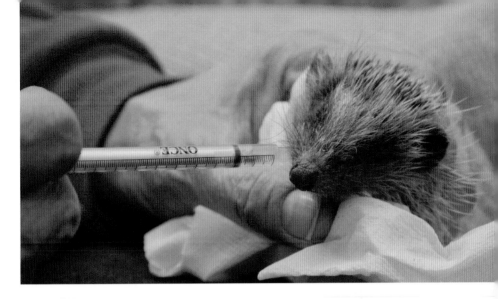

took in 6,002 animals of all species in 2018. Of these, by a very long way the most numerous was the hedgehog, with 1,130 casualties. They have an amazing and dedicated team who are on call 24 hours a day, 365 days a year and are able to cope with shrews and deer, swans and goldcrests, grass snakes and toads.

Another example is the Shepreth Wildlife Conservation Charity, which runs a small hedgehog hospital beside the Shepreth Zoo in Cambridgeshire. Here the efforts are focused on just the one species, despite there being armadillos, aardvarks and tigers next door. They average over 500 admissions each year, with 2017/18 seeing a dramatic and exhausting 825. The charity is also very interested in research, collecting and storing parasites and monitoring the success of rehabilitation.

Most carers, though, are much smaller, and some just take on the nearly fit ones in preparation for release. Given that most of the damage hedgehogs suffer from is as either a direct or indirect result of our actions, the value of these carers is enormous, but there is still not enough data on how many hedgehogs are taken in around the country and the fate of those that are released.

Another wildlife research project may end up helping hedgehogs and also give better guidance to carers. Garden Wildlife Health was set up by the vets at the Institute of Zoology, part of the Zoological Society of London, discovering that some species were suffering and that the observations of members of the public were crucial in their understanding. For example, greenfinches started to disappear, with numbers falling 60% in just ten years.

The principal cause was a disease, trichomonosis, that had spread from its more traditional host, the pigeon, into the greenfinch population. Learning about this enabled new advice to be given to people who fed birds in their gardens about hygiene, so it is not impossible that there may be an element of the hedgehog population decline that could be explained by disease. The bodies of hedgehogs that are found dead in gardens are sent to the vets at ZSL, where they are autopsied and samples are stored. Details of how to do this safely can be found on the project's website.

Also looked at are the parasites that can infect the hedgehog, the most famous of which has given the hedgehog a rather undeserved reputation: the flea. The hedgehog is often dismissed as being flea ridden, and also the cause for infestations on cats and dogs after they have been seen sniffing around a spiky bundle.

However, this is bordering on 'fake news'.

The hedgehog flea, *Archaeopsylla erinaceae,* is species specific – it only lives on the hedgehog, hence the second part of the Latin name. While the fleas might jump off the hedgehog to explore a potential new host, they cannot survive on a cat or a dog, let alone a human. These are all very alien environments for the flea, but there is a good reason why the hedgehog has this reputation.

The hedgehog is most likely to be spotted during the day, simply because they are easier to see. Hedgehogs are nocturnal and, on the whole, if they are out in daylight, they are poorly. Sick hedgehogs have a greater parasite load than healthy ones, hence the reason why the hedgehog gained this unfair reputation. In addition, the hedgehog flea is moving through an environment where it is far more visible than, say, a rabbit flea that is buried under insulating fur.

Myths and Legends

Myths and Legends

As with the fleas, there are many hedgehog stories that have been accumulated into myth and legend from the Old World and throughout recorded history. While they were never a grand animal, they have always been there and played a part in the way we imagine the world.

The presence of hedgehogs in the Bible surprises some – though it does depend on which translation you choose. The same verse (Isaiah 34:11) from the part known as the 'Judgement of the Nations' is translated in the following editions:

'The desert owl and the screech owl will posses it' (New International Version).

'But the hawk and the porcupine shall posses it' (English Standard Version).

'But pelican and hedgehog shall posses it' (New American Standard Bible).

'But the cormorant and the bittern shall posses it' (King James Bible).

The hedgehog is also referred to in Zephaniah (2:14) as the destruction of Ninevah was prophesied and is featured on an elegant bas relief on Amiens Cathedral in France in the context of that story.

The story behind the hedgehogs that appear on the misericord in New College, Oxford, though, is less easy to fathom. Here there are two, with a female centaur wielding an axe. That aspect remains a mystery, but there is something else in the carving that can be unravelled a little more. The hedgehogs have both got what would appear to be grapes stuck to their spines, and this is one of the long-

Above: Mysterious misericord from
New College chapel, Oxford.

lasting and utterly false stories about hedgehogs – that they collect fruit on their spines to store up and eat over the winter.

Hedgehogs do not collect fruit on their spines, nor do they store fruit to consume over winter. This claim that was written up as 'natural history' by Pliny the Elder in around AD 77, building, as he did so often, on the work of Aristotle. A translation of Pliny's work contains this compelling tale:

Hedgehogs also lay up food for the winter; rolling themselves on apples as they lie on the ground, they pierce one with their quills, and then take up another in the mouth, and so carry them into the hollows of trees... when they conceal themselves in their holes, afford a sure sign that the wind is about to change from north-east

to south. When they perceive the approach of the hunter, they draw in the head and feet, and all the lower part of the body, which is covered by a thin and defenceless down only, and then roll themselves up into the form of a ball, so that there is no way of taking hold of them but by their quills. When they are reduced to a state of desperation, they discharge a corrosive urine, which injures their skin and quills, as they are aware that it is for the sake of them that they are hunted...

[Hunters] force it to unroll itself, by sprinkling warm water upon it, and then, suspended by one of its hind legs, it is left to die of hunger; for there is no other mode of destroying it without doing injury to its skin... If it were not for the quills which it produces, the soft fleece of the sheep would have been given in vain to

mankind; for it is by means of its skin, that our woollen cloth is dressed.

There is so much in Pliny's tale, with elements of fact hidden among outrageous fantasy. Apart from the observation that hedgehogs roll into a ball when threatened, the other fact is that the spines were indeed used to card wool, which is just one of many interesting uses to which the hedgehog has been put. Hedgehogs have formed a staple of folk medicines across their range. In Ancient Egypt they were reputed to cure baldness, either in association with a hedgehog-shaped amulet or by using hedgehog oil, made by rendering the fat of a hedgehog ready for hibernation, one would assume. Ceramic hedgehog-shaped oil containers were in use in Egypt, with the earliest dated at around 1550 BC. Greeks of the seventh century

BC were also fond of the alleged curative properties of this oil and it continued into Romani medicines, where it was used to treat deafness. In England, during the 18th century, there were remedies where roasted and powdered hedgehog were used to treat kidney stones.

Pliny's assertion that hedgehogs collected fruit can be understood perhaps more so than some of the wilder ideas. Hedgehogs will undoubtedly have been seen rootling among the fallen fruit on the floor of an orchard or vineyard in the autumn, and the assumption will be that they are there to eat and collect fruit, but the reality is that they will be themselves feasting on the invertebrates that are feasting on the fruit. In someway, the fruit does provide for a hedgehog's hibernation, but only indirectly.

As for carrying fruit on their spines, this is harder to understand, as even the most simple of experiments will show that it does not work.

Imagine a happy hedgehog walking beneath a vine or plum tree, and a piece of fruit falls – the spines are all lying flat and it will not become impaled. Imagine a grumpy hedgehog all curled up beneath said fruit tree – should a soft plum fall and land on the hedgehog, it might become impaled, however, as soon as the hedgehog started to walk, it would drop off. Despite this being something that has never been witnessed, it is a story that has ended up being illustrated in many bestiaries.

Similarly, the long-running story about hedgehogs needing to be fed milk comes from another

Above: Medieval bestiary depicting hedgehogs collecting grapes.

misappreciation of reality. Hedgehogs are lactose intolerant, the problem being that they just don't know that, and will drink cows' milk when it is provided, sometimes to ill effect. But where would the idea come from?

If you look at the worm-chomping teeth of the hedgehog and the size of the teat of a cow, you can see that this was never going to work, but, early morning cud-chewing will often have the cows recumbent. In this state they may well seep a little milk, which would be attractive to a passing hedgehog, and when the herder came to round up the cows for milking, a culprit of theft would be in evidence with a milky face. As a result, people started to kill hedgehogs in an attempt to stop them stealing milk and the idea that milk was their favourite was born.

The killing of wildlife to help protect our own food supplies has a long and disagreeable history and the hedgehog really was down for execution. In his depressingly insightful book *Silent Fields* (2007), Roger Lovegrove analyses parish records over many years and reveals the extent to which the public were encouraged to kill, including the payment of bounties.

Hedgehogs would have been killed anyway, as what we now describe as 'bushmeat'. Traditionally, they were the diet of travelling people, but it is hard to believe that they would not have been utilised when other foods were in short supply. The act of cooking a gutted hedgehog wrapped in clay is not a myth, and is a suitable technique, though they can equally well be butchered and added to a stew. These days, it would be difficult to justify the act of eating anything other than fresh roadkill hedgehog, which a few people still do.

There is a great deal of prejudice about the relationship between the people of China and their wildlife, so it is a surprise for some to learn that around Beijing, for example, the hedgehog was considered one of four sacred species, along with the fox, weasel and snake. It was not all of each species that was sacred, there was skill needed to be able to identify the sacred from the profane, which could be hunted, but woe-betide anyone who interferes with a sacred individual.

This has not stopped the hedgehog from being subject to unnecessary assault, with some people breeding them for Traditional Chinese Medicine, despite TCM not having a use for hedgehogs. There are many instances where folk remedies get combined into the mainstream, in this instance to the detriment of the hedgehog. One, a Daurian hedgehog, was found being offered for sale in Chuzhou, Anhui Province, among a wide mixture of other wildlife, including centipedes and spiders.

Perhaps the grandest of hedgehog myths is where the humble animal is instrumental in the creation of the world as we know it. This Romanian story has a god finishing creation and realising that he has made a smooth orb with no room for the water. In confusion, he sends the bee to consult the wisest of creatures, the hedgehog, but the hedgehog is grumpy and tells the bee to go away. The bee, knowing the hedgehog is prone to muttering, lingers and hears, 'God does not know that he needs valleys and mountains in order to make room for the water. He must pick up the earth's skirts and create them.' And so, thanks to the hedgehog, we have the world as it is.

More modern folklore is emerging around the hedgehog, and in the USA there is a celebration of Groundhog Day – made famous by a film of that name – when, on 2nd February, a groundhog is presented to the assembled crowds at Gobbler's Knob, just outside Punxsutawney in Pennsylvania, as the sun rises. The tradition holds that if there is a shadow, it means that there will be a further six weeks of winter; however, a cloudy and overcast day tells all that winter is near an end.

But where did this quaint tradition come from? Well, there is a body of hedgehog pet keepers in the USA who are determined that this is a direct translation of an ancient Roman practice that was known as Hedgehog Day, with the same weather-predicting skills attached to the shadow of the hedgehog. So convinced are they of this that the date is now deeply inscribed into their calendars as Hedgehog Day and is associated with all sorts of prickly frivolity. It is, however, not true, on any account. There is no correlation between shadows and winter and there is no evidence that there was ever a Hedgehog Day in Rome, but where else do these stories come from but the imaginations of people!

Art, Literature and Advertising

Art, Literature and Advertising

The hedgehog has never been a glamorous animal of art, but it has always been there. The earliest civilisations have left us ceramic reminders of hedgehogs – Babylonians, Sumarians, Ancient Egyptians – all had a fascination with the animal. But why? That is where we risk drifting back into myths and legends.

There are a few ideas, however, that might account for the ancient hedgehog interest. Firstly, here is an animal that hibernates, or very likely aestivates, which leads to it becoming all but dead to the untrained eye. In a culture that had an interest in reincarnation, maybe this would be significant, or perhaps it is the ability of the hedgehog to survive an encounter with a snake. Certainly, the ceramic rattle hedgehog is considered to possibly be a snake deterrent, though the ability of the hedgehog to survive is less to do with magical properties and more to do with the length of the snake's fangs when compared to the hedgehog's spines! A snake attacking a hedgehog will find itself prickled and, if this enrages the snake, it will repeat. It has been known for the hedgehog to tolerate this for a while before starting to eat the snake, from the tail.

Or maybe the images are there because children would be able to play with a hedgehog thanks to its lack of fight or flight response, and these creations were simply toys?

Right (top): Hematite Babylonian seal from 20-16th century BC. Right (bottom): Egyptian Middle Kingdom hedgehog from 1900-1800 BC.

This humble animal has managed to generate its own version of philosophical thought – twice! In Ancient Greece, the poet Archilochus coined this aphorism: 'The fox knows many things, the hedgehog knows just one good thing.' The idea is simple – the fox is clever, it will try many different ways to eat the hedgehog, but the hedgehog, well, it has one good defence against the assault, and it uses it wisely. Clever foxes, wise hedgehogs.

This was good enough in itself but it was Isaiah Berlin who published an essay in 1953 that still feeds headlines to this day: *The Hedgehog and the Fox: An Essay on Tolstoy's View of History*. The central idea to this was to try and work out a theory that described the way people considered history and, further, how they thought about life in general.

A more erudite work it would be hard to find, but the essential theme is that there are two overarching ways of viewing the world of ideas or history. There are those who grasp a single big idea and associate everything with that view – these are the hedgehogs. Foxes, on the other hand, pursue many ideas. The essay proved to be a springboard from which much other work has been borne. It is most often applied to politicians and entrepreneurs, but most people probably see themselves as more one than the other.

The discussion is clearly summarised in this note from the journal *Neuroethics and International Biolaw*:

'A hedgehog is focused on one thing and sees unity, a fox, on the other hand, is focused on many things and engages in distinctions. Put another way, a hedgehog believes that education should be 'an inch wide and a mile deep'. A fox, on the other hand, believes that education should be 'a mile wide and an inch deep'.

The other leap into philosophy comes from Arthur Schopenhauer who, in his book *Appendices and Omissions* (1851), created the idea of the 'hedgehog's dilemma'. Two hedgehogs are cold, so they cuddle up for warmth but hurt each other with their spines, so they back off and get cold again. The dilemma is clear – how to be as close to each other without causing pain, and this, Schopenhauer asserts, is the perfect metaphor for human love. In getting close to the one we love there is vulnerability and pain, so the reaction is to push away into loneliness, until that can be tolerated no more and we head back into pain. Cheerful stuff.

While the hedgehog is now thought of as the most charismatic of creatures, that has not always been the case. In fact, in Britain, prior to the great change of 1905 and the appearance of Mrs Tiggy-Winkle, most stories associated with the hedgehog have painted it as an animal of portent or doom, and this is, perhaps, reflected in the Gaelic names which call it the 'horrible one'.

Shakespeare

Shakespeare, for example, references these charming animals twice. In *Richard III*, Act 1, Scene 2, Gloucester, prior to his coronation, is abused by Lady Anne calling him a hedgehog:

Dost grant me, hedgehog? then, God grant me too
Thou mayst be damned for that wicked deed!
O, he was gentle, mild and virtuous!

And in *A Midsummer Night's Dream*, Act 2, Scene 3, our favourite animal is cast among the other low beasts:

You spotted snakes with double tongue,
Thorny hedgehogs be not seen;
Newts and blindworms, do no wrong,
Come not near our fairy Queen.

The most disturbing hedgehog to make it into print has to come from the collection of the Brothers Grimm. In their telling of 'Hans My Hedgehog' we are presented with an animal/human hybrid who, while being dreadfully mistreated, does terrible things as well.

Famously, hedgehogs make a fairly passive appearance in *Alice's Adventures in Wonderland* (1865)

Albertus Seba, hedgehog from
Thesaurus rerum naturalium,
1734–65.

Konrad Gesner, hedgehog from
1551–57.

Right: Shoreditch street art by
Belgian artist ROA.

as croquet balls who do nothing to make this already fiendish game any easier. And then, the remarkable transformation that came with Beatrix Potter's tall tale of a washer-woman hedgehog. From that moment on the stories about hedgehogs have been almost exclusively featured a benign character.

Alison Uttley's stories featuring Fuzzypeg the Hedgehog in the 1930s were very much about a kind and simple character and in T.H. White's *The Once and Future King* (1958) the hedgehog is servile and simple. Enid Blyton got into hedgehogs with her *Hedgerow Tales* and the delightful *The Careless Hedgehog*. Molly Brett's *The Untidy Little Hedgehog* from 1967 still has the hedgehog as gently dim.

There are stacks of children's books featuring hedgehogs – perhaps most famously Dick King Smith's *The Hodgeheg*, which remains a staple for primary school classes. Picture books galore include *Princess Kalina and the Hedgehog; The Hedgehog Leaves Home; Pinny's Holiday; Hedgehog in the Hall; The Princess and the Hedgehog; Hedgehugs; The Happy Hedgehog Band; The Winter Hedgehog; The Untidy Little Hedgehog; The Hedgehog Feast; The Hedgehog's Balloon; The Three Hedgehogs; Samson le Herisson; The Carrels Hedgehogs* – and this is only a random selection from the shelf.

And they have also made it into books for older children too – most interestingly with Richard Mayer's *Spikez* (2012), featuring a robo-hog armed with an array of dangerously engineered super-spines.

One of the most popular poets Britain has ever produced was John Clare – this hedgerow genius wrote the following in the 1820s:

The hedgehog hides beneath the rotten hedge
And makes a great round nest of grass and sedge
Or in a bush or in a hollow tree
And many often stops and say they see
Him roll and fill his prickles full of crabs
And creep away and where the magpie dabs
His wing a muddy dyke in aged root
He makes a nest and fills it full of fruit...

It is telling that the 'observation' of the hedgehog collecting crabs (apples, not crustacea, that really would have been unusual) is kept at one remove from himself, as he clearly never saw it happen, because it doesn't happen.

IIn fact, hedgehogs have appeared in so many poems that the British Hedgehog Preservation Society produced an anthology in 1992 called *Prickly Poems*. This volume is a rich delight of words and images, but they are far from the only poems featuring them out there.

I am not convinced that Henry Wadsworth Longfellow was an expert zoologist as he inserted hedgehog quills into 'Hiawatha's Wedding Feast' when describing Pau-Puk-Keewis:

He was dressed in deer-skin leggings, Fringed with hedgehog quills and ermine,

Hedgehogs are not a native of the Americas – only having made their way over there in the late 20th century thanks to the exotic pet industry. And then, those are not 'our' hedgehogs – which are pointedly unsuitable for domestication – but smaller species from Africa.

Thomas Hardy, in 'Afterwards', reflects on legacy – how we could be remembered after death:

If I pass during some nocturnal blackness, mothy and warm, When the hedgehog travels furtively over the lawn, One may say, "He strove that such innocent creatures should come to no harm, But he could do little for them; and now he is gone."

Right: Fundraising collection of poems.

In association with the
BRITISH HEDGEHOG PRESERVATION SOCIETY

PRICKLY POEMS

An anthology of hedgehog poems

One of the most poignant of poems comes, perhaps surprisingly, from Philip Larkin. The story in *The Mower* is not for the faint-hearted and should be part of the teaching pack given to council workers who maintain amenity grassland. Though its concluding is one of the most poignant – 'we should be kind While there is still time.'

Ted Hughes, perhaps surprisingly, did not write a poem with a hedgehog at its heart, though he did write with great care and tenderness about a hedgehog he rescued in his letters.

More upbeat is the amazing *Luv Song* from Benjamin Zephaniah:

I am in luv wid a hedgehog
I've never felt this way before
I have luv fe dis hedgehog
An everyday I luv her more an more,
She lives by de shed
Where weeds and roses bed
An I just want de world to know
She makes me glow.

I am in luv wid a hedgehog
She's making me hair stand on edge,
So in luv wid dis hedgehog
An her friends
Who all live in de hedge
She visits me late
An eats off Danny's plate
But Danny's a cool tabby cat
He leaves it at dat.

I am in luv wid a hedgehog,
She's gone away so I must wait
But I do miss my hedgehog
Everytime she goes to hibernate.

Most recently, though, the hedgehog poet of choice has to be the inimitable Pam Ayres. Her original hedgehog poem, featured in *Prickly Poems*, does not bring her much joy, but *The Last Hedgehog*, published in 2018, is a wonderful work. When she launched the Oxfordshire campaign, HedgeOX, she completely lulled the packed audience in the Natural History Museum with a few funny lines and a general air of being everyone's favourite aunt, and then she started to recite the poem, by the end of which adults were crying.

With wit and pathos she managed to capture the key messages of the Hedgehog Street campaign in a short book of a poem, and in addition she also donated the advance she received to the BHPS – here is an excerpt:

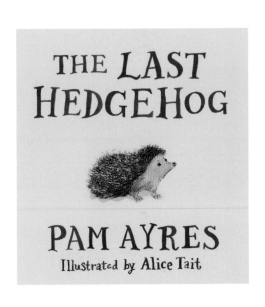

From now on, as you pull the drapes
You'll see no round familiar shapes,
Nevermore from dusk till dawn
Will we eat slugs on your lawn,
So little gratitude you've shown
From now on your can eat your own.

Hedgehogs have not been frequent in song, but they have appeared occasionally and if one searches on the internet there are two that will pop up. One is the beautiful and sweet composition of Mike Heron and played by the Incredible String Band – the other is x-rated, written in response to Nanny Ogg, a character in Terry Pratchett's Disc World novels.

This led to some confusion when former Archbishop of Canterbury Rowan Williams was invited on to the BBC Radio 4 programme Desert Island Discs. One of the eight records he chose was the *Hedgehog Song*. When his press team looked through the list there was a moment of panic, as the only example they knew was the rude one. Fortunately, he was a fan of the Incredible String Band.

Max Reger composed a sequence of songs about animals and included among them a lyric from Ernst Ludwig Schellenberg that is rather less kind towards the hedgehog, describing him as 'a bad fellow'.

The lyric is worth seeking out in the original German and references another view of the hedgehog that is not as benign as it is known and loved in Britain.

A more romantic image of the hedgehog can be found in the work of the Turkish artist Elvan Alpay, who has created large canvases of repeating hedgehog motifs in a lushly organic form. Though she has noted that they are largely absent in the iconography of her home country.

Right: From the exhibition 'Kirpi' (Hedgehog) by Elvan Alpay.

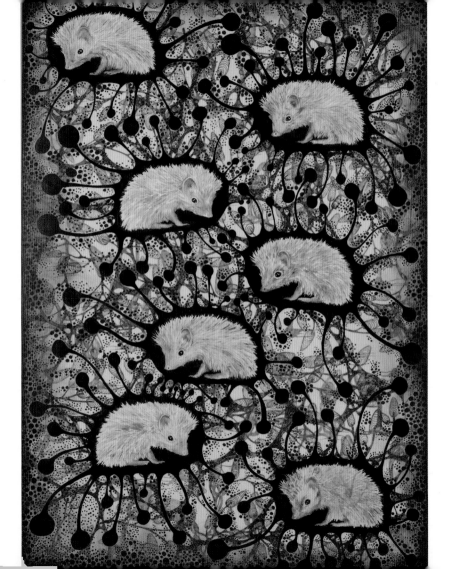

123

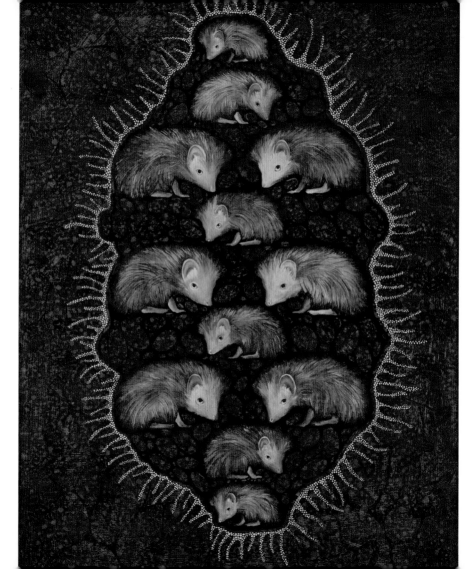

Advertising

Given the devotion displayed towards hedgehogs, it is not surprising to find that the animal has become a regular in advertising. Interestingly, there has been a fairly consistent association between hedgehogs and alcohol in recent years, ranging from the 1980s adverts for Côtes du Rhône to the magnificent Hobsons Brewery in Shropshire, who created 'Old Prickly' and donated to the BHPS for every pint and bottle sold. Now the mantle for hedgehog-supporting booze has gone to the delicious HedgePig Gin!

Left: From the exhibition 'Kirpi' (Hedgehog) by Elvan Alpay.

Possibly the most exciting hedgehog/alcohol cross over (should that hedgegrog?) was found in France, where, in the town of Herrison (yes, that is French for hedgehog) there is a distillery that produces Hedgehog whisky. On tasting, one reviewer described it as the most unpleasant liquid they had ever tried to consume – which is rather a shame.

Germany also has a town called Hedgehog – or Igel – which raises the question of why Britain, a country that loves the hedgehog far more than any other, judging by membership of similar organisations, has no town called Hedgehog. The closest seems to be unlikely at first – the Herefordshire town of Ross-on-Wye. Around 1500 years ago, when the land was occupied by the Celts, it was known as Ergyng, the land of the hedgehog, and in the church there, St Mary's, there are at least 14 of them to be found today.

There followed a series of names that all reflected the idea of 'hedgehog field', though it is easier to understand when you consider it as 'urchin-field'. In 915 in the Anglo-Saxon Chronicle there is 'Ircingafelda'; in 1086 the Domesday Book gives 'Arcenfelde'; in 1150 there is 'Herchenefeld', and on to 1679, when there is a reference to 'Urchenfeld'. The 'arc' is thought to possibly be a transcription error, as there is a consistency for many centuries with 'urch' or 'irch', both of which are clearly linked to our urchin.

Perhaps there needs to be a renaming of an old town to Hedgehog? Or possibly one of the newly suggested garden cities should receive such a name.

The hedgehog that is used in adverts in the UK is often, however, the wrong species. This leads to grumpy letters being sent – examples include Sega, when advertising a Sonic the Hedgehog game, who used four hedgehogs crossing a blue and white zebra crossing, complete with lollypop lady, but used three pet hedgehogs. When Ribena made a hallucinogenic advert about all things British, they failed to include a British, well, European hedgehog. And John Lewis, one year, had wildlife bouncing on a trampoline in an advert, in a very British and domestic setting, including a hedgehog that was quite clearly of the wrong species.

Above: Ancient door in Ross-on-Wye.

Banks have used the hedgehog, and rather disturbingly so have the manufacturers of car tyres, but perhaps the most ironic use of the hedgehog was by the Department of Transport, who for many years

Above and right: Hedgehogs in Ross-on-Wye church.

TO THE GLORY OF GOD
THIS MONUMENT WAS ERECTED
BY THE OFFICERS NCO° AND MEN
OF B CO°. 1ᵗʰ H.R.V. IN MEMORY OF
THE MEN OF B CO° WHO LOST THEIR
LIVES IN THE SOUTH AFRICAN WAR.

1901.

Pᵗᵉ E.H. ADAMS. | Pᵗᵉ J.P. SMITH.

Above: Decorated cappucino from Ross-on-Wye.

Right: Hedgehog ornament.

chose the hedgehog as the species of choice to educate children as to how best to cross the road. The only hedgehog that many of these children would have seen would have been dead on the roads, so this does seem to be presenting very mixed messages.

Back to Sonic – this computer game was originally released in 1991 and through its various iterations it has shifted around 800 million units and amassed an eye-watering $9 billion for Sega. Originally the plan had been for Sonic the Rabbit, but the developers in Japan just could not make the rabbit charge effectively enough, given the limitations of early computing power. Adding the spines gave the character an air of combat and hence was born Sonic the Hedgehog.

Pet Hedgehogs

Pet Hedgehogs

Historically in Britain, there is evidence that people would keep a hedgehog in their cellar to help control insect pests, but these would not really be characterised as pets, and our hedgehog, the European species, is not suited to domesticity.

However, back in 1991 an exotic pet dealer spotted some cute looking hedgehogs in a cage in West Africa and brought them over to the USA to see if there was a market. Suddenly, a new fad-pet was born and for the first time since the Miocene some 5 million years ago, hedgehogs were to be found in the Americas. Many thousands were imported until that was stopped for fear of disease.

As with all fad-pets, interest waned. This is, after all, a spiny nocturnal mammal that will run for hours at night on a wheel and on which they will poop, resulting in a shower of faeces that needs to be washed off before petting can begin. Some are very sweet natured, though, and they have certainly found a way deep into the hearts of many people, as exhibited by the Rocky Mountain Hedgehog Show, which takes place every two years in Denver, Colorado. A weekend of judging which is the cutest hedgehog culminates in the International Hedgehog Olympic Games – which is in fact more of a triathlon – with the hedgehogs taking part in the spring, hurdles and floor exercises. This has now been renamed the International Hedgehog Gymboree to avoid any suggestion of endorsement by the more traditional Olympic committee.

There are repeated attempts by exotic pet dealers in the UK to try and engineer a similar craze, with

money to be made if it takes off, but there are real and valid concerns. If this becomes something that promises reward, less scrupulous folk will take 'our' hedgehogs out of the wild and sell them to the unsuspecting. This would be very cruel for the hedgehogs and an additional threat to them in the wild. Additionally, it creates a shift in attitudes towards the natural world, turning it into a commodity – something to be bought and sold rather than valued in its own right.

For any African hedgehogs bred and sold in the UK, there is the risk of abandonment, as the psychological block on releasing an unwanted exotic pet into the wild is lessened, given our native population. This will result in either the inevitable death of the individual or them turning up in wildlife hospitals, where they will have to be kept and maintained, as they cannot be released into the wild.

The British Hedgehog
Preservation Society

The British Hedgehog Preservation Society

In 1982, Major Adrian Coles found first one, and then more, hedgehogs dead after becoming trapped in cattle grids. He started putting bricks inside the grids to allow hedgehogs to climb out and escape and recognised that this would not have been just a local problem. He started a campaign which, with coverage in the media, blossomed into the creation of the Society, and also resulted in the design of ramps that should be installed in all new cattle grids.

From small beginnings, the charity has grown considerably. There are now over 11,000 supporters who receive a delightful newsletter twice a year along with the famous 'Hogalogue'. This captures just some of the many eccentric hedgehog-related items that it is possible to buy for you or your hedgehog-loving friends. There is more to the BHPS than trinkets and cattle grids, however.

They have long been involved in campaigning to help hedgehogs, whether that is taking on fast-food giants or, in 2003, confronting the plans to kill hedgehogs in the Uists. These islands in the Outer Hebrides had hedgehogs introduced in the early 1970s and they were later accused of causing drastic declines in the breeding success of ground-nesting birds due to their taste for eggs.

The argument from the BHPS was not that the hedgehogs should be left alone; it was well recognised that there was a conservation issue to be dealt with, namely whether it was necessary to kill the hedgehogs. With serious dedication and many years' work, the society managed to persuade the conservationists that moving the hedgehogs would be just as effective as killing them, and this is still ongoing.

In 2007 the society was fortunate enough to receive a bequest from Dilys Breese, a BBC natural history film-maker who had worked on a documentary about hedgehogs with Pat Morris in 1982. She also left money to the People's Trust for Endangered Species with instruction that it should be spent on the betterment of our hedgehogs. It was at that point that the two charities joined forces, recognising that we could do far more good working together.

From this was born the campaign Hedgehog Street and also the joint funding of wide ranging research projects around the country. These have included, to date, 5 PhDs and

11 other studies and resulted in the publication of over 20 scientific papers.

This evergrowing body of work is a testament to the generosity of donors, large and small, who continue to enable the best scientists to try and understand how hedgehogs can be helped.

Recent work has included the training of Henry, a very clever spaniel, to find hedgehogs. This has given a great boost to researchers and also to those wanting to remove them from a site prior to builders moving in with bulldozers.

Hedgehog
Pat Morris

The BHPS has also been involved in funding the Hedgehog Officers at Wildlife Trusts around the country. Their role, working at the more local level to deliver hedgehog conservation messages and action, has been instrumental in increasing the awareness of the need to help the animal throughout the country.

Encouragingly, the roles have been highly sought after. When the post for Suffolk's Hedgehog Officer was advertised, it made the national and international news, resulting in hundreds of applications coming in from all over the world!

In the UK, the *Daily Telegraph* created an exciting advert for the post: 'Are you looking forward to going home after work today? And are you a bit bored of your job? You definitely wouldn't have this feeling if your job title was Hedgehog Officer.'

Meanwhile, *Time Magazine* ran with the headline ''Hedgehog Officer' Is a Real Job and This Town Is Hiring' (July 2016).

There are, of course, thousands of people doing some of the work of a Hedgehog Officer all the time around the country. Volunteers who go into schools and talk to children, individuals who notice a planning application that could destroy valuable hedgehog habitat and write in and the carers who give up hours to nurture hedgehogs back to health.

Pat Morris summarises the importance of the hedgehog in his latest book, *Hedgehog* (New Naturalist series):

'It is a popular creature that elicits sympathy and virtually no hostility. It is an ideal flagship species to carry forward important ecological and conservation principles to a broad public and encourage ordinary people to become involved with wildlife in their own personal environment. Moreover, what is beneficial to hedgehogs on the ground is also good for a wide range of other species to which most people would never give a thought.'

The 11,000 registered supporters are joined by many thousands of others who follow the society on social media, visit the website and contact them by phone to learn more about how to help our hedgehogs.

Over 10,000 phone calls are answered annually, and the website has over 100,000 unique visitors each year, while over 50,000 people wait eagerly for hedgehog tweets from the society and 200,000 are followers on Facebook.

The most frequent calls are from people wanting to know what to do with a sick or injured hedgehog, and while there is plenty of advice on the internet about this, there is reassurance from speaking to a human.

In most instances the advice is straightforward – get the hedgehog safely into a cardboard box. It will need food, water and warmth. Meaty pet food in a shallow dish or jam jar lid – similar with water. Warmth can be supplied by creating a hot water bottle out of a large drinks bottle, or setting the box on a more traditional hot water bottle. It is advisable to line the box with newspaper, as their faeces can be quite wet and they are notoriously messy eaters. Also include a towel or some other cloth that you are happy to wash at a high temperature.

Once secure, the hedgehog can be given a more thorough checking over. There is nothing more frustrating for the BHPS than to have someone call in having seen a hedgehog 'sunbathing' and then find that when they go to put it in the box, it has vanished.

The most common problems are around hedgehogs being found out in the day. These nocturnal mammals can and do move around in daylight, though not often. If you see a hedgehog on the move – purposefully crossing the lawn – during the day, leave it be. However, any hedgehog that appears to be either drunk or sunbathing, they are in trouble. Additionally, if they are being beset by flies, this is a bad sign.

More dramatic injuries just need to be treated with common sense. Get the hedgehog to safety, safely, and call the BHPS, who can direct you to the nearest hedgehog carer.

Helping individual hedgehogs is obviously important, but it is the work on the wider environment that will benefit them the most, and sees the BHPS involved in work to help the conservation of the species and in the removal of threats.

One way has been the idea of hedgehog road signs. Occasionally, individuals have taken this into their own hands and erected warning signs where hedgehogs have been seen run over. All it needs is for nocturnal motorists to just take a little more care and reduce their speed from 30 to 20mph in suburban areas. Not just hedgehogs benefit from this; it will make the environment safer for children, cats, and other wildlife.

Our love of the hedgehog enables us to manage our environment in a way that benefits so much more – and with that, we benefit too.

The idea appealed to the Minister at the Department of Transport, Chris Grayling, and he managed to push through a new road sign before his departure from office. Maybe it will become his lasting mark – a sign to warn drivers of the smaller mammals that need to be able to share this space.

The sign is a first; previous signs, showing images of deer and toads, are warnings about the risk to human life these animals present – colliding with a large animal like a deer or a boar is seriously detrimental to all parties concerned, and toads, well, it is unfortunate that the sign is there to warn motorists of the skid hazard that a mass of migrating toads create as they move to ancestral breeding ponds.

While the signs have a hedgehog as the image, they are not just warning about our little friend but about all smaller mammals, and this is a reflection on the importance of the hedgehog. It is the nation's favourite animal. People truly care about the hedgehog, but whether it is a hole in a fence, a wild patch in a garden, a park managed with hedgehogs in mind, or a road sign encouraging careful driving, all of these things seem to be for the hedgehog but actually help so much other wildlife too.

Our love of the hedgehog enables us to manage our environment in a way that benefits so many animals, and with that, we benefit too. The more wildlife we see, the better we feel, and there is nothing that makes you feel better than seeing a hedgehog.

Hugh Warwick

This is his fifth book – which have not all been about hedgehogs! Other work includes *The Beauty in the Beast* – a natural history of Britain as told through the enthusiasm of wildlife obsessives – and *Linescapes*, which investigates the impact that habitat fragmentation has on the ability of wildlife to thrive.

He lives in Oxford with long-suffering wife, Zoe, and children, Mati and Pip, and really needs a dog.

Hugh Warwick is an author and ecologist. Ecological fieldwork gave way to journalism and he has written for many newspapers and magazines, mainly on wildlife and environmental stories. He is also a frequent commentator on television and radio, often in his role as spokesperson for the British Hedgehog Preservation Society.

Photo Credits and Artworks

Front cover: Alamy

Back cover left to right: Hugh Warwick, The British Hedgehog Preservation Society, Hugh Warwick, Hugh Warwick.

Hugh Warwick, pages 4, 7, 8, 11, 13, 13, 27, 47, 48, 51, 53, 54, 57, 60, 63, 64, 68, 71, 71, 74, 75, 82, 85, 86, 89, 90, 91, 93, 94, 95, 99, 114, 125, 127, 128, 129, 130, 131, 132-3, 134, 137, 138, 139, 142, 143, 154, 155.

The British Hedgehog Preservation Society, pages 10, 14, 15, 28, 31, 35, 44, 52, 67, 145, 149, 150, 153.

Jarlath Flynn, pages 156-7.

Zoe Broughton, page 154.

Pat Morris, pages 9 (top), 9 (bottom), 12, 20, 32, 62.

Nick Upton, pages 16, 21, 22, 25, 36, 76-7, 78, 81, 144.

Gerard Oonk, page 59.

Vale Wildlife Hospital, page 24.

Melany Ferdman, page 19.

Andy Robinson (Hedgehog Street), page 39.

Alan Lochhead (Hedgehog Street), page 43.

Diane Balmer, page 55.

Jane Russ, endpapers linocuts.

Every effort has been made to trace copyright holders of material and acknowledge permission for this publication. The publisher apologises for any errors or omissions to rights holders and would be grateful for notification of credits and corrections that should be included in future reprints or editions of this book.

Acknowledgements

Dr Pat Morris started the scientific study of hedgehogs and he is still key to our efforts to best conserve the species. Without him, I doubt I would be doing what I do now; his support has been invaluable. The CEO of the BHPS, Fay Vass, has become a very tolerant friend over many years of collaboration. Thank you to all of the team who make Hedgehog Street such a vibrant campaign.

This book would have been so much less interesting without the wonderful photographers who have let me use their work. In particular the amazing Nick Upton, who has developed his own unique techniques to capture hedgehogs in all their beauty.

And, finally, thank you to my wonderful family, who cope with a house filled with hedgehog artifacts. Zoe, Mati and Pip – I hope this will help explain what I have been up to in the shed for so long! You might think that three books on hedgehogs are enough... but there is another one brewing!

The Hedgehog Book
Published in Great Britain in 2020 by
Graffeg Limited.

Written by Hugh Warwick copyright ©
2020. Designed and produced by Graffeg
Limited copyright © 2020.

Graffeg Limited, 24 Stradey Park
Business Centre, Mwrwg Road,
Llangennech, Llanelli, Carmarthenshire,
SA14 8YP, Wales, UK. Tel: 01554 824000.
www.graffeg.com.

The publisher gratefully acknowledges
the financial support of this book by the
Welsh Books Council. www.gwales.com

ISBN 9781913134419

1 2 3 4 5 6 7 8 9

Books in the series

The Hare Book

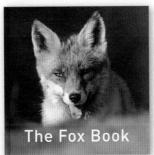
The Fox Book

The Owl Book

The Red Squirrel Book

The Bee Book

The Robin Book

www.graffeg.com

GRAFFEG